PENUMBRA LIGHT

PENUMBRA LIGHT

FRAGMENTS FROM THE GLEAM BEYOND THE GLOOM

BETHANY "LOREKEEPER" DAVIS

Grimr Press
Broomfield, Colorado

Grimr Press is an Imprint of Caer Illandria Publishing

Copyright © 2019 by Bethany "Lorekeeper" Davis. All rights reserved.

All poems dated with original copyright, © 2015-2019

"I Walk the Edges" and "The Cliff at the End of Time" reference the line, "Out here in the perimeter there are no stars." This line is from poetry by Jim Morrison, contained in "The WASP (Texas Radio and the Big Beat)," a song released on the album L.A. Woman, April 19, 1971

For information please address:

Grimr Press
P.O. Box 7557
Broomfield, CO 80021

books@grimrpress.com
www.grimrpress.com

Printed in the United States of America
First Edition

ISBN-10: 0-9986200-4-1
ISBN-13: 978-0-9986200-4-6

For the Hidden One, who rules the Outer Dark.

For DRGN, Rex Picti, a mentor, a friend, a twin twenty years removed. Though I met you in person only after death, your memory will always live on.

And most of all, for my Sophia, who walks all the paths with me.

CONTENTS

PENUMBRA LIGHT 3
IN THE GLEAM BEYOND THE GLOOM 5
ENDLESSNESS... 7
TWILIT LANDS 9
I AM THE RAVEN OF DREAMS... 13
I WALK THE EDGES... 17
THE CLIFFS AT THE EDGE OF TIME 19
WHERE WALK THE LOST AND DEAD 23
FOOTPRINTS FADE 27
THREE ALTARS I KNOW 31
WINTER SNOWS... 35
TEARS OF A THOUSAND SOULS 37
THE CITY OF STARS 39
THE THIEF OF MEMORY 43
THE STENCH OF ROTTING SOULS... 45
PALE ETERNITY... 47
QUEST OF THE WANE-FUL QUEEN 51
WHERE THE SERPENTS LIE 53
FOREVER SOARING FREE 57
THE SEVEN SCRIBES 59
THAT WHISPER 63
THE CONVERSATION OF THE ANCIENTS 67

I made an offering of wind upon the altar of dust.
— Sayings of the Grimr

Penumbra Light

Bethany "Lorekeeper" Davis

Penumbra Light

The parting Veil in penumbra light in the last pale light of day,
A mist that flows and moves all still floating ethereal in the dusk,
What is seen is all unseen, what's known is never known,
And what does wait through gossamer is far beyond all thought,
And in the dusk as sunlight fades and Night does not soar quite yet,
The Gloom is full, a living thing, full of nameless things.

The parting Veil in penumbra light in the last pale light of day,
Shifting shadows of the Gloom and things that should not be named,
Where the Lost on gypsy feet pass back and forth from here,
Some to be no more ever known and some to soon return,
And in the dusk as sunlight fades and Night does not soar quite yet,
The Gloom is full, a living thing, full of nameless things.

The parting Veil in penumbra light in the last pale light of day,
And dreams do walk on silent feet and nightmares roam about,
The sunset fades from red to blue and then onward to the dark,
And shadowed forms that aren't quite seen walk in ethereal light,
And in the dusk as sunlight fades and Night does not soar quite yet,
The Gloom is full, a living thing, full of nameless things.

The parting Veil in penumbra light in the last pale light of day,
The Gloom that is the wall and breach and gate to what is far,
The Gleam that knows eternal light and knows eternal night,
Where strange things walk and hunt and stalk and stay beyond the Veil,
And in the dusk as sunlight fades and Night does not soar quite yet,
The Gloom is full, a living thing, full of nameless things.

The parting Veil in penumbra light in the last pale light of day,
A mist that flows and moves all still floating ethereal in the dusk,
What is seen is all unseen, what's known is never known,
And what does wait through gossamer is far beyond all thought,
And in the dusk as sunlight fades and Night does not soar quite yet,
The Gloom is full, a living thing, full of nameless things.

~December 7, 2015

Bethany "Lorekeeper" Davis

In the Gleam Beyond the Gloom

Through the darkness I part the Veil,
And walk the hidden paths,
In the brightness beyond the pale,
I see what none have seen.
There's danger here in the world beyond,
In the gleam beyond the gloom.

And all my days it waits for me,
The calling in my blood,
And through the years I walk the paths,
That very few have seen,
The Veil grows thin as years go by,
In the gleam beyond the gloom.

Through the darkness I return again,
From those fair hidden paths,
And as I walk I learn to talk,
Like I once knew I could,
For few have been beyond the veil,
In the gleam beyond the gloom.

~March 5, 2015

Bethany "Lorekeeper" Davis

Endlessness

There's a sea of tears beyond the Gloom,
Out there within the Gleam,
A thousand tears from a thousand eyes,
Each year that's ever been,
On and on that endless sea,
That spans all of eternity,
Few eyes have seen the sea of tears,
But all have put it there.

There is a plain of endless hope,
Out there within the Gleam,
A thousand wishes have spread it wide,
Each thought of what might be,
On and on that endless plain,
That spans all of eternity,
Few eyes have seen the plain of hope,
But all have put it there.

There is a wood of fear and lose,
Out there within the Gleam,
A thousand fears on a thousand nights,
Each pain that could ever come,
On and on that endless wood,
That spans all eternity,
Few eyes have seen the wood of fear,
But all have put it there.

~May 22, 2015

Bethany "Lorekeeper" Davis

ר

Twilit Lands

The eternal plains are living things,
And the forests watch and wait,
The mountains sleep but always dream,
And the seas know all that is,
And the cliffs that dwell at the edge of time,
At the edge of eternal night,
Crumble forth and let water flow,
Like an infinity of tears.

The forest leaves that ever fall,
When Autumn never ends,
The winter snow on bare, bare limbs,
Of trees that ever sleep,
The green, green growth always new,
When Spring reigns eternally,
And through the endless Summertime,
When the Autumn never comes.

Out on the plains that never end,
That stretch to eternity,
Green in Spring and Summer gold,
Brown Fall and endless snow,
All of time that stretches on,
Just like the endless plains,
Forever onward the journey goes,
In the path that never ends.

The mountains rising forever high,
Past clouds that never end,
Snow-capped peaks forever cold,
And springtime flowers bloom,
The winter heat without a sun,
The autumn drying out,
The peaks forever changing time,
That never change at all.

Bethany "Lorekeeper" Davis

The sea is rough with Winter storms,
And calm with Springtime breeze,
The summer months when all the ships,
Work the endless tides,
In Fall they crash the Autumntide,
That never knows an end,
The endless seas just like the plains,
The journey never ends.

And on the cliffs that know no end,
That ever sour on down,
Waterfalls of hot and cold,
That never hit the ground,
The Tower rests where time resolves,
Just like the last long chord,
Where Autumn, Winter, Spring, and Summer,
Are one forevermore.

Across the plains and endless woods,
The mountains and endless seas,
The twilit realms than know all time,
And the end where time is not,
Where stars shone bright or never shine,
And shadows ever dance,
All the twilit lands are one,
And are a living thing.

~October 23, 2016

Penumbra Light

Bethany "Lorekeeper" Davis

I am the Raven of Dreams
A Poem of Candlemas

I am the Raven of Dreams,
Who wanders the dreamscapes of yore,
I pluck the thoughts and memories,
That aren't remembered no more,
Shiny things in thoughts and dreams,
And babbles of treasure lost,
In memories long faded away,
In dreams that will live on.

I am the Raven of Dreams,
Who wanders the dreamscapes of yore,
My beak will tear and rip and pull,
And feed on memory's corpse,
All is food to the one who calls,
And walks the dusk and dawn,
In memories long faded away,
In dreams that will live on.

I am the Raven of Dreams,
Who wanders the dreamscapes of yore,
And finds lost things that none could find,
And brings them home with me,
The babbles I seek I will always take,
To decorate my nest,
In memories long faded away,
In dreams that will live on.

I am the Raven of Dreams,
Who wanders the dreamscapes of yore,
Up mountains so tall that no one can climb,
But I can fly so high,
Across endless plains no one can cross,
But I can fly so fast,
In memories long faded away,
In dreams that will live on.

Bethany "Lorekeeper" Davis

I am the Raven of Dreams,
Who wanders the dreamscapes of yore,
Across endless seas where all become lost,
But I can fly so strong,
Through dark woods so dark no one can see,
But I can fly beyond,
In memories long faded away,
In dreams that will live on.

I am the Raven of Dreams,
Who wanders the dreamscapes of yore,
And finds the secrets among all our thoughts,
And finds out all there is,
The paths I fly no one can go,
The treasures are mine alone,
In memories long faded away,
In dreams that will live on.

I am the Raven of Dreams,
Who wanders the dreamscapes of yore,
I pluck the thoughts and memories,
That aren't remembered no more,
Shiny things in thoughts and dreams,
And babbles of treasure lost,
In memories long faded away,
In dreams that will live on.

~February 2, 2016

Penumbra Light

Bethany "Lorekeeper" Davis

ו

I walk the Edges

I walk edges,
Any label will fail,
And none have meaning,
Out at the perimeter,
Where there are no stars.

~April, 16, 2016

Bethany "Lorekeeper" Davis

ז

The Cliffs at the Edge of Time

There is a tower high above,
On the cliff at the edge of time,
Above the clouds its lighthouse shines,
Above the Abyss of yore,
And in the dark that was before,
The dews of creation came,
In the Outer Dark it lights the way,
To travelers few have known.

There is a tower high above,
On the cliff at the edge of time,
The shadowed lands, the stuff of dream,
That end at the endless cliff,
Stretch out behind its endless light,
A warning light as well,
For the light that guides the nameless things,
Warns away the things of time.

There is a tower high above,
On the cliff at the edge of time,
Lost in the endless eternal night,
Where the stars come to an end,
At that cliff the Gleaming ends,
So far beyond the Gloom,
The Outer Dark that waits beyond,
Is more endless than all of time.

There is a tower high above,
On the cliff at the edge of time,
The forgotten keeper tends the light,
A light that will always shine,
A shadowed folk who no one knows,
The loneliest who ever lived,
Who lit the light when the world begin,
At the edge of the Outer Dark.

Bethany "Lorekeeper" Davis

There is a tower high above,
On the cliff at the edge of time,
And few there are who visit there,
Or see the keeper's light,
A journey long across eternity,
A journey few can make,
At the edge of stars at the perimeter,
Where's found the Outer Dark.

There is a tower high above,
On the cliff at the edge of time,
The secrets there are as deep as time,
Or the souring endless cliff,
To know their words or what lies beyond,
Is a feat few could ever do,
For to understand their forbidden truth,
Is to taste the Outer Dark.

There is a tower high above,
On the cliffs at the edge of time,
The things there seen by the keeper's eyes,
Would drive the sane insane,
For few can look at eternal night,
At what lies in that old Abyss,
The forgotten things that make their home,
In the darkest Outer Dark.

There is a tower high above,
On the cliffs at the edge of time,
And the mists that rise from the endless depths,
Would make your blood run cold,
Only the light of the keeper's light,
Can pierce their endless cowl,
And guide the things beyond all fears,
Back from the Outer Dark.

Penumbra Light

There is a tower high above,
On the cliffs at the edge of time,
The echoes heard from the old Abyss,
Most ears could not withstand,
The keeper blind who sees so much,
And hears with deafened ears,
Knows the depths and lengths and the breadths,
Of the endless Outer Dark.

There is a tower high above,
On the cliffs at the edge of time,
Across endless plains and endless seas,
Woods and mountains that never end,
At the edge of that endless cliff,
Where time slowly slides away,
And when it's down not will remain,
But the tower and the Outer Dark.

~October 10, 2016

Bethany "Lorekeeper" Davis

Where Walk the Lost and Dead

There is a mist that seldom parts,
That is not fog nor normal mist,
It parts and opens forth beyond,
To paths where walk the Lost and Dead.

Shadowed lands beyond the Veil,
Ever shifting and never still,
Paths that are never just the same,
Those paths where walk the Lost and Dead.

In mist-filled vales and gloomy glens,
The lichen moves without a wind,
Each odd tree is never the same,
Between paths where walk the Lost and Dead.

The paths that lead through gloaming hills,
Ever changing like water trills,
Both the ways and still the traps,
Those paths where walk the Lost and Dead.

To Gleam they flow from Dreaming lands,
To Dream they flow from Gleaming lands,
Those paths that wrap and twist and turn,
Those paths where walk the Lost and Dead.

Bethany "Lorekeeper" Davis

The mist is thick sometimes or thin,
Swirling like a winter storm,
Misleading visions that lead astray,
On paths where walk the Lost and Dead.

There are things that wait within the mist,
And others in Dreaming and Gleaming lands,
Dangers out upon the way,
On paths where walk the Lost and Dead.

The endless paths that sometimes end,
Both where you want and where you don't,
It's easy there it lose your way,
On paths where walk the Lost and Dead.

All you that walk there will soon understand,
That there's not always a lost or found,
When you are walking through misty lands,
Upon paths where walk the Lost and Dead.

For there is a mist that seldom parts,
That is not fog nor normal mist,
It parts and opens forth beyond,
To paths where walk the Lost and Dead.

~January 30, 2017

Penumbra Light

Bethany "Lorekeeper" Davis

Footprints Fade

The sand stretches wide in twilit light,
Black sand like a thousand stars,
The stars above are oh so strange,
To eyes of the world we know,
These endless shores of eternity,
Black sand that never ends,
Between endless sea and endless plain,
In the Gleam beyond the Gloom.

The sea is strange to human eyes,
That only know Dreaming seas,
For they stretch beyond forevermore,
No horizon you'll ever see,
Endless seas of endless tears,
All the sorrow we've ever known,
Under starry skies in the Gleaming land,
Past that shore of endless sand.

And the plains they stretch just as far,
With their dunes and downs and hills,
The eyes don't like to see endlessness,
When the horizon is nowhere seen,
Grass it sways from a thousand winds,
On those plains that are our hopes,
Under starry skies in that Gleaming land,
'Fore that shore of endless sand.

And on that shore you can walk and walk,
But you'll never find a place to rest,
For that shore between the seas and plains,
Is not a shore that will ever end,
And so you walk on black, black sand,
Until you cannot walk no more,
And naught has changed on that endless shore,
Since your walk there first began.

Bethany "Lorekeeper" Davis

But in the sand where you walk and walk,
If you stop and look 'round and down,
Footprints fade in that black, black sand,
Of that endless winding shore,
And if you look and you truly see,
You are never quite alone,
That figure stands and it waits for you,
On that endless shining shore.

Shadowed face under ragged cowl,
Just a hint of what seems a skull,
And tattered rags over a weary form,
With tattered wings tucked behind,
Bone white hands with a faded book,
Where life and death are wrought,
And the silent tongue and silent form,
On that endless shining shore.

What you saw and what you recall,
Might not be just what you saw,
But the figure waits on that endless shore,
Waits in your recessed mind,
And starry light off of black, black sand,
On an endless winding shore,
Those footprints fade like memories,
From the Gleam beyond the Gloom.

~February 6, 2017

Penumbra Light

Bethany "Lorekeeper" Davis

י

Three Altars I Know

Three altars I know beyond the Veil,
In those twilit lands beyond the pale,
Three altars that stand since time began,
In the mist of the Gleam beyond the Gloom,
Three are the Veiled Ones who stand alone,
At those three altars that all time forgets,
Three altars I know beyond the Veil,
Three altars that stand 'til time is no more.

On the misty island where the spiders weave,
Where no one goes unless there is need,
One clothed in red and veiled in white,
Stands there at that altar where all things began,
Red is the altar that holds the forge,
Where the Spinner forges all things new,
Three altars I know beyond the Veil,
Three altars that stand 'til time is no more.

Deep in the forest where the shadows hunt,
Where no one goes unless there is need,
One clothed in white and veiled in black,
Stand there at that altar where all things change,
White is the altar where the tapestry spreads,
Where the Weaver weaves our hopes and dreams,
Three altars I know beyond the Veil,
Three altars that stand 'til time is no more.

Bethany "Lorekeeper" Davis

Deep in the mountains past the horn and bone gates,
Where no one goes until it's too late,
One clothed in black and veiled in red,
Stands there at the altar where all things end,
Black is the altar where the final blade falls,
Where the Cutter cuts the Threads in the fullness of time,
Three altars I know beyond the Veil,
Three altars that stand 'til time is no more.

Three altars I know beyond the Veil,
In those twilit lands beyond the pale,
Three altars that stand since time began,
In the mist of the Gleam beyond the Gloom,
Three are the Veiled Ones who stand alone,
At those three altars that all time forgets,
Three altars I know beyond the Veil,
Three altars that stand 'til time is no more.

~February 19, 2017

Penumbra Light

Bethany "Lorekeeper" Davis

כ

Winter Snows

A lady walks through winter snow,
Along eternal mountain trails,
Clad in a white and ice blue dress,
That trails behind her path,
All tracks are gone like from the wind,
None know when she has passed,
Just a chill as cold as death,
And thoughts of winter storms.

A lady walks through winter snow,
Along eternal mountain trails,
Ice crystals form on ancient trees,
As her shadow covers them,
Swirling snow like misty veils,
Dances around her form,
Bringing a chill as cold as death,
And thought of winter storms.

A lady walks through winter snow,
Along eternal mountain trails,
A lonely walk of one all alone,
The eternal silence of the lost,
How does it feel to walk the paths,
And never know friend or foe?
Solitude as cold as death,
All alone with winter storms.

~March 2, 2017

Bethany "Lorekeeper" Davis

Tears of a Thousand Souls

On the eternal sea, that sea of tears,
That all who weep should know,
Under endless stars that never set,
Where twilight will never cease,
On that black sand that stretches on,
Where death does walk the shore,
On that edge where the waves crash on,
The waves that will never end,
Til time does end as all things do,
When death's wings are finally spread,
There she sits, there all alone,
On the shore of the sea of tears,
Her ragged hair as dark as night,
Hair that's never known a comb,
A thousand strands of fate it is,
A thousand oily locks,
That hide her face like a veil of night,
Like that sky with the endless stars,
Ragged are the clothes she wears,
Pieced together from a thousand lies,
The secrets told and the ones untold,
Whether truth or cold false lies,
Her skin is pale like the white of bone,
Or the caps on the endless waves,
Her eyes so black like the raven's eyes,
Eyes so blind that see so much,
Gaze she does into the endless sea,
Reading the secrets of every tear,
And her own do fall to join the throng,
In that endless sea of tears,
She who walks the desolate places,
Who knows all the secrets known,
Cries the tears of a thousand souls,
Upon the shore of the endless sea,
And as her eyes at last run dry,
And all her tears are spent,
She takes the form of a thousand birds,
And the ravens fly back again.

~March 27, 2017

מ

The City of Stars

I've seen a city on a cliff so high,
Beyond the veil and gloaming gloom,
It is a city so hard to know,
In breadth or width or height,
Many souls, too many to count,
Live in that gleaming city there,
In the gleam beyond the gloaming gloom,
Where stands the city of the stars.

I've seen a city on a cliff so high,
Beyond the veil and gloaming gloom,
Where the endless sands come to an end,
Where black sands give way to high chalk cliffs,
Below the cliffs the waves crash on,
At the edge of the endless sea of tears,
And eat the cliffs and the end of sand,
Where stands the city of the stars.

I've seen a city on a cliff so high,
Beyond the veil and gloaming gloom,
The city spreads from east to west,
And from the north on to the south,
An endless city full of endless sights,
Where none can find the end,
Where the endless cliffs crash to endless waves,
And falls the city of the stars.

Bethany "Lorekeeper" Davis

I've seen a city on a cliff so high,
Beyond the veil and gloaming gloom,
Each wave it takes a sacrifice,
Of white cliffs and city fair,
But all the waves in the sea of tears,
Make the city not any less,
For it stretches on like the endless cliffs,
Where stands the city of the stars.

I've seen a city on a cliff so high,
Beyond the veil and gloaming gloom,
A cliff so high no man can climb,
Or even think to reach the heights,
And she who climbs has been climbing long,
She no longer remembers before,
But she knows she'll reach at the end of time,
Where stands the city of the stars.

~April 28, 2017

Penumbra Light

Bethany "Lorekeeper" Davis

ב

The Thief of Memory

In the City of Stars beyond the gloom, a single soul does walk,
Silent steps upon crumbling streets, no shadow does she cast,
All the crowds that mill around, in those endless, ancient streets,
In all those crowds not one soul stops, to note her passing by,
Small she is, much more than most, small and lithely built,
Like a ghost that walks the endless streets, beneath the endless skies,
Forever walking forevermore, until all that is have died.

How she longs for endless plains, or forests under endless skies,
But the city streets beyond the gloom, is where her feet do walk,
What she takes from other hands, none know that it is lost,
The memory of the things she takes, are but whispers in the wind,
Like a ghost that walks the endless streets, beneath the endless skies,
Forever walking forevermore, until all that is have died.

Memories stolen from city streets, beyond the paling gloom,
Like all the streets in dreaming lands, on this side of the pale,
When they pass beyond our grasping hands, and are stolen
    forevermore,
Lost for all our many lives, not to ever be found no more,
A ghost that walks the endless streets, beneath the endless skies,
Forever walking forevermore, until all that is have died.

- September 4, 2017

Bethany "Lorekeeper" Davis

The Stench of Rotting Souls

In the twisted woods beyond the veil,
Where all our fears find their final tale,
There is a wood that's worse than most,
Where a thousand thousand trees do stand,
A copse of corpses it might be termed,
A rotting place that shall never burn,
Trees of grey under storm black sky,
Hence weathered leaves fall for all time,
Leaves sickly grey like rotting flesh,
Half-old leaves like of autumn's end,
Down they fall from the nameless heights,
Of a thousand thousand dying trees,
Down and down to the ground below,
They fall like sickly grey dead snow,
To the shadowed ground so far below,
Where things do move forevermore,
Things the watching eyes wish unseen,
The moving forms of soul-torn flesh,
A thousand thousand corpses move,
Not living now but still they squirm,
With sticky blood from a thousand wounds,
Blood turned black in the solemn dread,
A thousand wounds on the once dead flesh,
And guts hang down from sinew threads,
Each organ moves and pulses strange,
And clotted blood flows evermore,
The gory sight brings all to fear,
And the sound that comes is worse so near,
But of the stench no bowels can hold,
The sickening putrid smell of deathly mold,
From a thousand thousand rotting souls,
The corpses found in the dark grey cold,
Forever crawling with their gurgled cries,
The smell so bad off the crows do fly,
And leave the corpses to crawl in peace,
Under a thousand thousand grey old trees,
And leaves that fall already dead,
Under stormy night of unhallowed dead,
Where all our fears find their final tale,
In the twisted woods beyond the veil.

~September 9, 2017

Bethany "Lorekeeper" Davis

Pale Eternity

I see a graveyard across rolling hills,
A graveyard that knows no end,
On it stretches on all around,
As far as any eye can see,
An endless graveyard on that endless plain,
That stretches to the endless sea,
Each gravestone blank in the twilit light,
The dead forgotten in pale eternity.

Each gravestone rises each unique,
Like placid sun bleached bone,
A story lost in the winds of time,
Some from back from when time began,
What secrets there in silence rest,
Tales that none can hear,
Each gravestone blank in the twilit light,
The dead forgotten in pale eternity.

Black dark trees as dark as night,
Stand as leafless sentries,
Barren cypress and dormant yew,
As if winter holds them close,
Ribbons tied upon each branch,
Offerings to the lost and dead,
Each gravestone blank in the twilit light,
The dead forgotten in pale eternity.

The ancient city that knows no end,
That endless City of Stars,
That stands upon the cliffs of time,
Above the endless sea of tears,
The countless ones who have walked those streets,
Are few compared to the sea of graves,
Each gravestone blank in the twilit light,
The dead forgotten in pale eternity.

Bethany "Lorekeeper" Davis

The countless crows that fill the trees,
Bare branches with ribbons and birds,
The ravens dance on endless graves,
In a most sacred menagerie,
The echoing caws of the countless crows,
Mix with the countless raven calls,
Each gravestone blank in the twilit light,
The dead forgotten in pale eternity.

The gates of death are very close,
To every sun bleached grave,
Beneath the loam in that endless place,
In that cavern so deep below,
Where at that black altar a figure stands,
And beyond another keeps the gates,
Each gravestone blank in the twilit light,
The dead forgotten in pale eternity.

I see a graveyard across rolling hills,
A graveyard that knows no end,
On it stretches on all around,
As far as any eye can see,
An endless graveyard on that endless plain,
That stretches to the endless sea,
Each gravestone blank in the twilit light,
The dead forgotten in pale eternity.

~February 4, 2018

Penumbra Light

Bethany "Lorekeeper" Davis

Quest of the Wane-ful Queen

Through hidden glens and hollow hills,
And across the rolling loam,
They make their way in twos and threes,
A rambling roaming mob,
On horses strange with eyes of fire,
And hel-ful hunting dogs,
Their falcons soar with hungry eyes,
That seek a living soul.

Forth they come behind their queen,
From places twixt and tween,
A trooping court in search of blood,
A court that hunts for flesh,
Their quarry lives in towns and homes,
Living so unaware,
And whom they find will breathe their last,
Upon this world we share.

Wild they ride upon this hunt,
Each eye that looks for blood,
A queen of ice in summer heat,
Leads forth the dogs of war,
Onward come the wane-ful throng,
The wild questing hunt,
Not for white hart or wild hind,
It's for as all they hunt.

Like a wave of bloody gloom,
The folk of gloam they ride,
The dust like froth left in their wake,
Blood red behind the throng,
They make their way in twos and threes,
A rambling roaming mob,
Through hidden glens and hollow hills,
And across the rolling loam.

~June 14, 2018

Bethany "Lorekeeper" Davis

Where the Serpents Lie

In a lonely valley far away,
Amongst the endless peaks,
Far above the endless plains,
And endless stretching woods,
In that valley lost among the clouds,
Hides a silent mountain lake,
In a place no eye has ever seen,
And seen anything else again.

No sound breaks that mountain calm,
Not for centuries in a stretch,
And hunger grows through endless days,
Where that lonely water waits,
Until someone finds that place,
And finds out what hunger waits,
In a place no eye has ever seen,
And seen anything else again.

The shrieks that echo across the lake,
Makes mortal blood run cold,
And drives away the silent calm,
And brings fear to every heart,
The hunters come from all around,
The trespasser there to kill,
In a place no eye has ever seen,
And seen anything else again.

Bethany "Lorekeeper" Davis

Coiled bodies like giant snakes,
Move faster than lighting strikes,
And hands that snatch and teeth that tear,
Flesh from more bleeding flesh,
And eyes that shine with endless light,
As they seek the food that came,
In a place no eye has ever seen,
And seen anything else again.

When naught but blood is all that's left,
And all have had their fill,
Their serpent coils slowly move away,
And their teeth hide back inside,
And as they go to sleep once more,
The silence settles in,
In a place no eye has ever seen,
And seen anything else again.

~July 22, 2018

Penumbra Light

Bethany "Lorekeeper" Davis

Forever Soaring Free

Across the sea of endless waves,
Wings tirelessly part the air,
Crystal clear the waters stretch,
Black sand beneath the waves,
And clouds that sail like many ships,
Right upon the rolling waves,
What is fog so far below,
Like islands from the sky.

The wings that soar have always been,
And will always part the air,
On and on just like the wind,
Above the rolling endless sea,
Never turning from the course,
Not up nor down nor o'er,
Forever flying straight ahead,
Upon those endless winds.

The endless waves they never cease,
Just like the endless skies above,
Rolling above the endless sands,
Beneath that rolling endless sea,
The pitch black sands of memory,
Beneath the endless sea of tears,
Forever rolling on and on,
Like the tireless wings above.

The thing that flies and soars above,
Has no memory but the sea,
Forever soaring without end,
Forever soaring free,
But what freedom lives in endlessness,
In never knowing change,
Above the endless rolling waves,
Above the sands of memory.

~June 22, 2019

Bethany "Lorekeeper" Davis

ר

The Seven Scribes

In that place beyond the mist,
That's everything there is,
Beyond the Gloom beyond the Veil,
In the Gleam that never ends,
Seven scribes record the deeds,
Of all that have ever lived.

One scribe sits on the highest peak,
Of the mountains that have no end,
Among the clouds too high to know,
The scribe records the deeds,
Of every dream that's thought or done,
No matter how hard to reach.

One scribe sits in the endless woods,
Below the endless peaks,
Among the roots in shadows deep,
The scribe records the deeds,
Of every fear that cools the heart,
No matter how hard to face.

One scribe sits the endless hills,
Near the endless trees,
Among the graves of eternity,
The scribe records the deeds,
Of every death that came about,
No matter who was left behind.

One scribe sits on the endless plains,
That stretches forevermore,
Among the grass that forever waves,
The scribe records the deeds,
Of every hope that every was,
No matter how hopeless they might seem.

One scribe sits on the endless shores,
Between the plains and sea,
Among the black and endless sands,
The scribe records the deeds,
Of every memory found or lost,
No matter how hard to recall.

One scribe sits among the endless sea,
On an island among the waves,
Surrounded by those endless crests,
The scribe records the deeds,
Of every sorrow that was ever felt,
No matter how hard to bear.

One scribe sits on the endless cliffs,
Where the endless sea waves end,
And those falls at the end of time,
The scribe records the deeds,
Of all that's lost or never was,
At the edge of the Outer Dark.

In that place beyond the mist,
That's everything there is,
Beyond the Gloom beyond the Veil,
In the Gleam that never ends,
Seven scribes record the deeds,
Of all that have ever lived.

~July 2, 2019

Penumbra Light

Bethany "Lorekeeper" Davis

That Whisper

There is a wind, as cold as death,
That blows between the worlds,
It whispers there, in every ear,
In every waiting world,
This wind it speaks, of many things,
Things beyond all of belief,
Of things that may have never been,
And things that will always be,
But the cold wind moves, that fickle thing,
Moves on when we think we hear,
And leaves us behind, still wondering,
If that whisper was even real.

There is a wind, as cold as death,
That blows between the worlds,
It blows on by, that lonely tower,
On the cliffs at the end of time.
It whispers there, right in the ear,
Of the keeper of that light,
And it listens hard, and hears those thoughts,
That the keeper never speaks,
And in the whisper, of that fickle wind,
The secrets are spread all wide,
But we don't recall, if we heard those words,
Or if that whisper was even real.

There is a wind, as cold as death,
That blows between the worlds,
Across the sea, that sea of tears,
That sea that never ends,
The sea it speaks, of all the things,
All of us have ever cried,
And the cold cold wind, it hears them all,
And carries them away,
And so it speaks, of all our loss,
And all our laughing tears,
But no one knows, what it is it says,
Or if that whisper was even real.

Bethany "Lorekeeper" Davis

There is a wind, as cold as death,
That blows between the worlds,
Across plain of hopes, where all our dreams,
Run wild, strong, and free,
Our dreams they speak, and share their hope,
And the wind goes rushing by,
And listens well, and hears just fine,
What is in every dream,
And so it tells, to all it sees,
The secret hopes of dreams,
But no one know, what it was they heard,
Or if that whisper was even real.

There is a wind, as cold as death,
That blows between the worlds,
Across the woods, where all our fears,
Are waiting to find a voice,
And when they speak, they speak of us,
From our deepest and darkest souls,
And that fickle wind, it hears them there,
And it collects them as it goes,
And all along, it calls them out,
To everyone it finds,
But few there are, that remember it,
Or if that whisper was even real.

There is a wind, as cold as death,
That blows between the worlds,
Across the peaks, that never end,
Our ambitions and our goals,
That rising peaks, so old and still,
That speak in slower words,
What we want, and how we strive,
And what we want to do,
But still blows on, that fickle wind,
And listens to all that's said,
But we don't recall, what was said,
Or if that whisper was even real.

Penumbra Light

There is a wind, as cold as death,
That blows between the worlds,
It blows across that Black Altar,
Where every thread is cut,
And the red veiled form, dressed in black,
Who welds that cutting blade,
It blows on by, the tattered robes,
Of the one before the Gate,
And blows beyond, through the Gates of Death,
And back through the Gates of Life,
Of death it speaks, and of life,
If that whisper is even real.

~February 1, 2017

Bethany "Lorekeeper" Davis

ת

The Conversation of the Ancients

The voices echo through the halls of time,
And through all the worlds and years,
The ancient voices from before it all,
And from when all that has been is gone,
The words are strange but ever known,
By all things that have ever lived,
The heartbeat of all the many worlds,
That echoes through living threads,
Ancient voices from the outer dark,
Beyond the endless sea and cliff,
Speaking secrets that are known to all,
In a language that none have known,
In time their speech grows very loud,
Or drops to a whisper few can hear,
The ebb and flow that is the eternal beat,
That fills all the breadth of time,
The speech is that which can drive you mad,
Or fill the poets with eternal words,
The song of life and song of death,
The song of what has never been,
The halls of time echo with the words,
And the threads of fate ring strong,
With the ancient words that ever ring,
Through endless waves beyond,
And when all that is has finally ceased,
As if naught that is now had been,
The conversation of the ancient ones,
That rang long before time began,
That song that will never again be known,
Will ring on still in the endless night.

~July 10, 2017

Bethany "Lorekeeper" Davis

ABOUT THE AUTHOR

Bethany "Lorekeeper" Davis, also known as Muninn's Kiss, currently resides in Colorado, near Denver, in the Dreaming at Plains Edge. She lives there with her true love, her Sophia.

She is the founder of Grimr, a tribe member of Toteg Tribe, a practitioner of the 1734 stream, and a student of Anderson Craft.

She is the proud mother of a fey creature in the form of a cat, adopted mother of a bird in the form of a cat, is a part time vegan and part time meat connoisseur, and a walker of edges.

Her life pursuit is to find beauty, knowledge, understanding, and wisdom in all things. Bethany has been writing poetry and prose most of her life, among other pursuits.

www.ingramcontent.com/pod-product-compliance
Lightning Source LLC
Chambersburg PA
CBHW030456010526
44118CB00011B/963